Dan Taylor

A Second Dissertation on Singing in the Worship of God

Introduced with two letters to the Revd. Mr. Gilbert Boyce, in defence of a former dissertation on that subject

Dan Taylor

A Second Dissertation on Singing in the Worship of God
Introduced with two letters to the Revd. Mr. Gilbert Boyce, in defence of a former dissertation on that subject

ISBN/EAN: 9783337290580

Printed in Europe, USA, Canada, Australia, Japan

Cover: Foto ©Lupo / pixelio.de

More available books at **www.hansebooks.com**

SECOND DISSERTATION

ON

SINGING

IN THE

WORSHIP OF GOD;

Introduced with

TWO LETTERS

TO THE

Rev^d. Mr. *GILBERT BOYCE*,

In DEFENCE of

A former DISSERTATION on that Subject.

By DAN TAYLOR.

" Musical Sing is most agreeable to praising and adoring God."
CYPRIAN.

LONDON:
Printed for J. BUCKLAND, Paternoster-Row; and
B. ASH, No. 15, Little Tower Street. 1787.

LETTER I.

To the Reverend Mr. *Boyce*.

SIR,

IT is my opinion that you have made several mistakes in your late *Reply* to me; but I think, not one more flagrant than when you say, (p. 17.) " the subject of singing is a favourite topic with me." If I may be allowed to judge of my own feelings, I scarcely know any subject that is less my favourite topic than this; nor can I imagine why you call it such. When I have been among such as omit this practice, have I discovered any peculiar uneasiness because of that omission? Did I ever introduce a controversy about it? Will any of my correspondents say that I ever discovered a fondness for this subject? I believe not. But, among the few observations of my short life, I have frequently made one, viz. " When men assume the divine prerogative in judging the hearts of others, they often make great blunders." You have, in the present instance, confirmed this observation.

I do not know that I ever undertook any work more unwillingly, than the writing of my *Dissertation on Singing*, not because I am doubtful whether the practice can be fairly supported; but for several other reasons, which need not now be mentioned. Being persuaded, however, that duty called me to it, I opposed my inclination; and put a few plain things together, as they, at that time, arose in my own mind, which, I thought, might place the subject in an easy and profitable light.

Although the publication of your *Serious Thoughts* was the *cause* of my writing on the subject, yet it was by no means, my *chief design* to answer what you had written. I only intended to take notice of what appeared to me argumentative in your piece; and to intersperse remarks on that, with my own thoughts on the subject. And I wrote in the dissertation form, as that appeared to me least inimical to you; and not so likely to hurt your feelings by treating you as an antagonist. It appeared to me that your *Serious Thoughts* laid a foundation for *vain jangling*, which I wished to avoid; and I am sorry to observe that your late *Reply* appears directly calculated to answer the same bad purpose.

In your *Reply*, as well as your *Serious Thoughts*, you must confess, and all men will see, there are many things which do not affect the argument. Many of these must, for the sake of decency, as well as brevity, be quite passed over in silence. Your, "Ah, my brother, are you not gotten on the wrong side of the question?—what a dilemma have you brought yourself into!" and a great number of other little despicable things, far beneath the regard of any thing that wears the shape of a man, shall be as though they had never been. But there are some other things on which justice to myself, to our readers, and to the subject, requires me to animadvert, though they have no immediate relation to the point in question. What relates to the subject, and may be considered as argumentative, I reserve to the next letter. And with regard to the whole, I appeal to all who know what they read, and have any understanding of the rules of disputation, or of decency, whether you have not laid yourself open in a very uncommon degree, in many places which I entirely pass over; and of which I might otherwise avail myself to expose you, that were my inclination. When I speak thus, I refer to *both* your performances.*

* The contents of this letter, I am sensible, has no necessary connection with the question in hand, between Mr. B. and me, nor do they prove that Mr. B's

The limits I have just now prescribed to myself, include your title page, which contains many curious articles, and which has, I doubt not, afforded considerable entertainment to no small number of your readers. *Some* of these require present attention. You call your performance a *Reply* to my Dissertation. But ought not a *replier* to consider the arguments of his opponent; and either to acknowledge the force, or prove the futility of those arguments? Can you imagine that any impartial man will admit that you have done this? You call it " a *candid* and *friendly* reply:" but do you think your readers will call it so? "The whole now submitted to the consideration of the Christian world at large." Why, Sir,

B's hypothesis is erroneous: but every intelligent reader will observe the necessity of them, to vindicate my own character, as well as that of multitudes, from the aspersions implied in my friend's insinuations, as well as to excite caution in the unwary reader. Nothing but a conviction of their necessity in this view, could, I think, have prevailed with me to undertake so disagreeable a task. But things of this sort ought, by no means, to be mingled with the argument. I have therefore given them a place here by themselves, that the reader might not be diverted, or any other way improperly influenced, when he comes to the subject in dispute. Every man of understanding must observe, that I have left many unbecoming parts of Mr. B's performance unnoticed; and my conscience bears me witness, that if it had been consistent with a due regard for truth, I should be glad to cover them all with the mantle of love.

is not every book thus submitted? may not any man read and consider it? You can hardly mean that such puny performances, as your's and mine, shall have the honour to travel over any considerable part of the Christian world. Do you mean that you invite the whole Christian world to read it, and challenge them to answer it? Suffer us not to have such an idea of your modesty. " More especially Protestant Dissenters." Why these more than other people? why, because they are such, and ought to act consistently. For by this same *Reply* " it appears they ought to renounce *all human authority* in matters of Christian *faith* and *worship*, or otherwise, return to the *bosom of the national church.*" This supposes that the Protestant Dissenters do *professedly* practise singing on the ground of *human authority*. And is it a *fact*, Sir, that the Protestant Dissenters practise singing on this ground? If it be a fact, why do you confront them with scripture? So far as any man professes to act on this principle, he has no business with scripture, either to vindicate or refute him. And if the Protestant Dissenters do not profess to sing on this ground, is the imputation implied in these words *equitable*? Would it be *fair* to insinuate that you act from human authority, when you plead the authority of both the Old and New Testament in favour of your practice?

practice? If not, please to read and think of Mat. vii. 12. Again, " By which it *appears*, they ought to renounce all human authority, &c." By which what, Sir? by which *reply*, to be sure. By what part of it? I cannot find any thing like such an *appearance* in any page of your Reply, nor so much as a hint about it. Certainly, you forgot the design of your book, as soon as you had written the title page. But I omit the rest, and venture to put it down as my private opinion, that your title page, and your contemptible puff *to the public* in the page following, compose one of the completest pieces of folly and abuse, which has been produced in so short a compass in the present age.

I thank you, Sir, for your recommendation of my *Consistent Christian*. As the mistakes made in your quotations from that piece are possibly owing to your printer's negligence; I only say, I wish he had taken more care. With your usual generosity of temper, you frequently hold up that piece to my view. I should be sorry to find that any *candid* and *friendly* man has reason to complain of my deviation from it, on this or any other subject.

You begin your " *Candid* and *Friendly* Reply," at p. 9. and in the four following pages, as well as frequently afterwards, you throw out slurs and insinuations hardly
consistent

confiftent with *candour* and *friendſhip*. But to take notice of all theſe would be of little uſe to ourſelves, or our readers. In p. 14, 15. however, you come directly home, and charge me with ſpeaking againſt you—with injuſtice,—unfairneſs,—reſolution to expoſe you,—and even untruth; which, to be ſure, are heavy charges; and if well founded, deſerve the reſentment you have manifeſted.

Now, Sir, the proper way, as I conceive, to vindicate myſelf fully from theſe charges, would be to tranſcribe many pages of your *Serious Thoughts*, and the few lines which you have cited from my Diſſertation; and, as there are ſo very few who read with attention and underſtanding, to reaſon upon them, and demonſtrate the juſtneſs of my *hints* from the current language of your *Serious Thoughts*. But ſo much of this ſtuff would be an intolerable affront to the intelligent reader. I muſt therefore ſubmit, and I do cheerfully ſubmit to ſtand at the bar of the public, and to abide by their deciſion. If much of the language of your *Serious Thoughts* be not what I have repreſented it, I fall, and I fall juſtly; for ſuch I ſtill aſſert it to be; and I appeal to all ſenſible men for the truth of it.

To tell me that theſe things "never came into your heart," Sir, is to do nothing. I did not write about your *heart*, but your book;

book; and by your *book*, not your *heart*, I am to be judged. "Have you ever known me," say you, "to be the man you have represented me to be?" Why, Sir, what kind of man have I represented you to be? I did not represent you as a *man*; but as a *writer*. The hints I dropped did not respect the *man*, but his performance. I never mentioned you as a *man*, but with expressions of esteem and respect. I spoke of the " hoary head found in the way of righteousness;" which is one of the noblest of characters. This I applied to you; and this I firmly believe you deserve. I called you " my aged friend, (p. 15.) a venerable man, (p. 28.) an aged minister of Christ, and a good gentleman, (p. 45.) These, with some slighter and more indirect expressions of esteem, (p. 28. 42.) were, I think, all which I said about you.

I confess, I detest the manner of your writing, without any regard to the subject; for I should have viewed it in the same light, and thought it a scandal to the cause of truth, had I believed the things you have written, as I do not. Yet I value and esteem you as a *man*; and in this view, should be ashamed to speak or write one word to your disadvantage. Nor am I singular in my censures. I think all the intelligent part of my acquaintance, who have given me their opinion, are of the same judg-

judgment with myself respecting your manner of writing. And I find that you yourself have met with others, who see it in the same light. Witness p. 74 of your *Reply*.

I can, with great sincerity, assure you, that a regard for your age and character, a fear of hurting your mind, and an unwillingness to expose you, were among the reasons of my reluctance to write on singing. Had your *Serious Thoughts* been written by a *young* man, I believe I should have thought it my duty, in hopes of doing good to others as well as himself, while I pitied his vanity, to have treated him with freedom; and to have chastised his insolence with a proper degree of severity. But when I considered who was the author, I thought it sufficient gently to intimate, that we were not entirely void of sensations.

I happened to intimate that you had called " our practice of singing" by many *ugly* names. (Diff. p. 50.) You demand proof of this. (Reply, p. 15.) Your demand is certainly very just. For to utter a syllable to the disadvantage of another, without being able and ready to authenticate the fact referred to, is not to be excused. What do you think then, Sir, of the following expressions? " Growing error;
" will-worship; singing the words of poets,
" or poetical men; a tottering fabric; the
" error of singing; the chains of set and
" prescript

"prescript forms of singing; downright disobedience; ear-pleasing singing; new invented way of singing; pleasing error; new invented exercise; formal service; scriptureless way of singing; a shameful and dishonourable custom; new invention; a glaring unscriptural practice, &c." *Serious Thoughts*, p. 5, 11, 12, 23, 24, 29, 33, 35, 37, 38, 42, 43, 45.

Now, Sir, please to consider that you were only opening the controversy — you had previously proved nothing—attempted nothing—yourself were the only aggressor—you write against a practice held sacred by all the Christian world in all ages, a very few excepted; so few, that they scarcely bear any comparison to the whole—against a practice held sacred by the greatest and best of men of all parties, and of all descriptions. Consider this, and then say, if there be any great *beauty* in these expressions. I readily grant that you have a right to vindicate your own practices and sentiments as well as all other men; and, if you please you have a right to oppose all mankind, and to set up yourself as dictator to " that great *community* the Christian world." But, surely, unless " you be the man, and unless wisdom shall die with you," a little modesty becomes you: and a little consideration would have convinced you, that

to

to infult men is not the way to inftruct them.

I endeavoured, as I thought, not to offend you in writing my Differtation; and therefore omitted a great many things, the mention of which might have had that tendency. Yet it feems I have had the misfortune to offend you exceedingly, even to fuch a degree, as you intimate, (p. 15.) that I cannot, in prefent circumftances, be indulged with the honour of fhaking you by the hand. You do me the pleafure, however, to propofe an expedient, and thereby to inform me that you are not quite implacable. I thank you, good Sir, for this inftance of condefcenfion. But I am ftill embarraffed. The price of your friendfhip is too high. I cannot poffibly reach it. It is not in my power to " wipe of" what you call " the afperfions which I have fo liberally caft upon you." As I am very fure that the hints I dropped were founded in truth, and not at all proportioned to the blame you deferved, I cannot retract them, left all thinking men, as well as my own confcience, fhould condemn me.——Still, however, I am encouraged to hope that you are " not my enemy." I truft, Sir, I fhall never be capable of flighting the friendfhip of any good man.—But you will " return good for evil." Nay, here, Sir, you overdo it. I muft now entreat you to

excufe

excuse me, and allow me to shut my hand. I cannot accept so great a favour as this from any man living. If you will fairly prove, before the face of the world, that I have done you any evil, I do, in this public manner, promise to make you all the satisfaction in my power, and publicly to beg your pardon for the rest. But I do scorn the meanness, and I hate the baseness of receiving " good for evil." To be quite free, Sir, however I esteem you in other respects, I sincerely despise this proposal; and, in this one view, I sincerely despise the man who was capable of making it.

In p. 17. you call upon me to prove four things. But what authority have you, Sir, to make this demand? Did I ever assert these four things? Who gave you a right to demand from me the proof of what I never asserted? You pay me high compliments on the " strong and forcible arguments contained in my other publications." But if any one should choose to attack me in your manner, on other subjects, he would soon prove me to be weak enough. He has only to bully, instead of reasoning; to substitute banter and brow-beating for argument; to pass over my reasonings (if such they be) and say, these " are not worth my notice; this is nothing to the purpose; that proves nothing;" and so on. He can quote part of an argument instead
of

of the whole, leaving out that part in which the ſtrength lies; and then apply the reſt to a ſubject different from that to which I applied it, and cry out of its weakneſs; and ſo begin to talk about " dilemmas, and wrong ſides of the queſtion;" and who in the world is able to ſtand before ſuch weapons, and ſuch warriors as theſe? How far this is juſt, will appear from the careful reading of your *Reply*, and in part, from the following pages.

Another paſſage of your *Reply*, which comes within the limits preſcibed to this epiſtle, is in p. 29, 30. You tell me, I " encourage and plead for *that*, which the great head of the church has no where commanded; ſo that all I have ſaid hitherto is of no validity." It is a ſufficient anſwer to this, to obſerve, that when you have examined my arguments (if they deſerve that name) and demonſtrated the invalidity of them, the public will probably be able to judge between us to more advantage. At preſent, your readers ſee that moſt of my arguments are not only unanſwered, but even untouched; and therefore this obſervation is rather premature. You add, " I think you lay yourſelf under ſome deſerved reproof." As to the validity of my arguments, there are thoſe, who think differently from you in this article; and I believe, unleſs you convince them of the contrary,

trary, they will continue to differ from you. This, however, is a point to be settled, when you have examined what I have said on the subjects in question. But why *deserved reproof*, Sir? Admitting you are in the right, do people *deserve reproof* for being mistaken, or for propagating what they believe to be truth? If persons deserve reproof from others for being mistaken, then all men will deserve reproof one of another; for we all think one another mistaken; and therefore, if you be right in this expression, we may all begin to reprove one another; and the whole world, without the exception of a single individual, must be engaged in broils and quarrels. If I deserve reproof, however, you certainly deserve commendation for paying me what is my due so liberally as you have done. But why, I venture to enquire again, why deserve reproof? Are we returned to Rome? Who has placed you, Sir, in the chair of his Holiness, to reprove those, who, in your opinion, are mistaken? To talk of any man deserving reproof, because he propagates what he believes to be right, however mistaken, is to strike at the root of the Protestant cause, and to attempt the establishment of that destructive principle, which is the very basis of popery. If I deserve reproof from you, I deserve, on the same principle, the gibbet, or the fire of

Smith-

Smithfield, from the civil magistrate. No argument can be produced to evince, that any man deserves reproof for publishing his religious sentiments, which will not equally vindicate and sanctify all the fines and the imprisonments, the racks, and the various tortures, the fires and the faggots, the halters and the gibbets, and every other diabolical invention which has been used to oppose the truth, and to suppress liberty of of conscience from the creation of the world to the present moment.

This seems to be a proper place to take notice of the consequences which you assert, (p. 62.) results from admitting, that our way of singing is right. "Then" say you, " all of us who do not sing in your manner, must certainly be bold and daring sinners against him who is King of kings, and Lord of lords." Now suppose the truth of this, what has that to do with the argument? But where is the truth of it? Are all mistaken persons bold and daring sinners? You know the principle, Sir, from which you wrote this, and many other parts of your *Reply*. But to examine that is not my province. A word is enough.

I do assure you, I am already heartily tired of trailing after you in this dirty channel. Your late performance would supply matter of this sort, to fill a large volume. But I beg to be excused from the drudgery
of

of gathering it up. I therefore only add, that you have thought it proper to hold out my profaneness to the world, as one who " allows of eating blood;" and have taken care, with your usual dexterity, to place it in the most conspicuous situation, by reserving it for your postscript: your motives here also have undoubtedly been long since conjectured by your readers; but these are nothing to me. I have nothing to do with the hearts of men. I may, however, be allowed to exculpate myself from the charge of such *heinous* crimes, so far as truth will permit. It is well known, and I should think you cannot be ignorant of it, that I both am, and, since I made a profession of Christianity, to the best of my remembrance, always have been, as cautious of eating blood as you yourself, though from a very different principle. The principle on which I abstain from it, is contained in Rom. xiv. 13—22. At the same time, I think a regard for truth requires me to observe, that it is my opinion the eating of blood cannot be proved to be universally and absolutely forbidden.

I conclude, by declaring, that while I take no pleasure in this idle squabble, I impute nothing to corrupt design in you; I leave every thing of this kind to him, whose prerogative it is. Whether your late publications are spontaneous productions,

or

or whether you are a tool in some bad hand, is best known to yourself. I pity your case. I very sensibly feel for you, and sincerely wish you well. I earnestly wish that you, and the handful of people who abet your opinion, may consider the importance of that interest which is almost dead among you, and of that precious gospel, which alone can preserve it from total destruction, and recover the vigour and credit of it; and that you and they may employ your time and abilities for that divinely glorious purpose. I do assure you further, that though shaking you by the hand is a favour too great for such a culprit as I am to obtain; yet my hand, heart, and house are always at your service, open for your reception, and ready to give every possible proof, that I am,

Dear Sir,

Affectionately yours,

DAN TAYLOR.

LETTER II.

To the Reverend Mr. *Boyce*.

SIR,

I am extremely sorry to find myself under the disagreeable necessity of appearing against you in the field of controversy as a direct antagonist. I earnestly wished to avoid it; and in my dissertation on singing, notwithstanding your challenges, I endeavoured to avoid it as much as possible, consistently with maintaining a proper regard for sacred truth. I therefore endeavoured to state my views of the subject as inoffensively as I could, only taking notice of what you had written, as it were, by the bye. This, I apprehend, clearly appears to every observant reader of our pieces. You have now thought it proper to make your attack directly upon me, as you did in your former piece on all who practise singing in public worship. As we are not, in this world, to have the choice of our own pleasures and crosses, I submit, and take the ground you have assigned me, so far as appears to me necessary, to vindicate what I assuredly believe is the cause of truth. In my former letter, I have cited a few a few passages out of a great many, in which your addrefs, and manner of treating an *adverfary*, appear to me highly reprehenfible. For liberty of confcience in propagating truth, is no licence to abufe one another, or for any man to infult his fellow-creatures. I am now, in a few inftances, to confider your manner of treating the *fubject*.

Your Reply begins at p. 9. where you confefs with me, that " finging the praifes of God is plainly and frequently recommended in the facred fcriptures." " And what then?" You enquire. I anfwer, nothing but what is there afferted. You faw I meant nothing more, than to prove this one point by exprefs fcripture. I did not here attempt to prove it a part of public worfhip; and therefore to oppofe that idea, in this place, is a manifeft impropriety.— To talk of " drawing arguments from the Old Teftament," is on two accounts unfair. —Becaufe I here drew no argument at all— and the texts I had quoted were from the New Teftament, as well as the Old.

Having adduced this clear and exprefs evidence in favour of finging, from both the Old and New Teftament, I enquired, (Diff. p. 11.) " Is it not the duty of thofe who oppofe it, to fhew where it is abrogated, and where the bleffed God has appointed it to be laid afide?" You anfwer, " No:

"No: I think not." But I think you are certainly mistaken. Singing is an ordinance of both the Old and New Testament; circumcision is only an Old Testament institution. But now, suppose a Jew were to argue in favour of circumcision, and Jewish rites; would not you think it necessary to shew him that these were peculiar to the Jewish œconomy, and are therefore to be laid aside at the commencement of Christianity? Certainly you would. And thus we reason in every similar case. Every institution continues in force till the time when the institutor appointed that it should cease. No man can safely omit what God has appointed as a duty, unless he can shew that the appointment is now of no force. As to the *manner* of singing which you go on to speak of, you here *knew* that was not the matter in question. I had particularly mentioned it only three lines before, to prevent the blunder you have made. (See Diff. p. 10, 11. Reply, p. 15, 16.) If we wish "to prove that we ought to sing," how can we do it more fully than by producing the express commands of both Testaments? I enquired, 2dly, "Whether it is more becoming a Christian to perform it as well as he can, than pass it over in neglect?" "I think," you reply, "it is much better not to do a thing, than not to do it according to the will of God." I answer; singing

singing is strictly enjoined by the blessed God himself, both under the law and the gospel. This I had fully proved. The express passages were before your eyes. Nothing can therefore excuse the neglect of it, unless we can shew that the institution is not now in force. This, I believe, no man can do. It therefore certainly behoves every Christian "to perform it as well as he can."

You and others have frequently spoken of singing in divine worship as pleasing to carnal people. This you frequently glance at in your *Serious Thoughts*.——With reference to which I observed, that the practice is recommended as excellent, not only in the judgment of carnal men, but of God himself. "This comparison," you reply, " of the judgment of carnal men of the *excellency* of singing, with the judgment of the all-wise and most holy God; shocked me when I read it." (Diff. p. 11. Reply, to p. 18.) But why this out-cry? why so much shocked? Is *but* a note of comparison. Suppose you were to tell one who is an enemy against Christianity, that " Jesus is the Son of God," is a truth believed, not only in heaven, *but* in hell too; not only by angels, *but* also by devils. Would that be a *comparison* of hell with heaven, or of devils with angels? would it not be a plain and undeniable truth? And do not you yourself confess the truth of what I here said,

though

though you tell the world the reading of it *shocked* you? Do you attempt to disapprove it? will any man attempt it, who believes the Bible? If not, pray, Sir, reflect on the spirit and design from which this observation arose.

In p. 20. you enquire, "If God does not give his good Spirit to any in these days, to qualify them to sing, as they were qualified for that service in the apostle's days; where have we authority to set up in the church what sort of singing we please?" Is this *fair*, Sir? is this insinuation according to the golden rule? (Mat. vii. 12.) Do we pretend to that authority? Did you find any such pretence in my Dissertation?—I ask farther, Does "God give his good Spirit to any in these days to qualify them to *preach* and to *pray*, as they were qualified for these services in the apostle's days?" You will not pretend it. What then? must praying and preaching be laid aside? or are we at liberty to pray and preach as we please? You know very well, and must confess, that praying, preaching, and singing are all enjoined in the New Testament. Ought we not then to practise them all as well as we are able?

I endeavoured to prove that singing the praises of God was not peculiar to the Jewish dispensation. Ought you not to have considered these proofs? You know
thi

this is a point of confiderable importance to determine the controverfy. Was it *candid, friendly, fair*, to pafs them by? (Diff. p. 21, 22, 23. Reply, p. 25.) One argument I mentioned on this head, was, that "the New Teftament is not only filent with refpect to the abolition of it; (finging) but inculcates and enforces it, both by precept and example." This argument you take up thus, "The New Teftament inculcates it both by precept and example." —You leave out the main claufe in the argument, where the chief weight lies. And then "inculcates and enforces what? the Jewifh finging as above? How do you prove it?" Now, Sir, could you imagine, could any one imagine that I had regard to the Jewifh finging, at the very time when I was profeffedly proving that finging was not confined to the Jewifh church? I muft afk again, Is it the part of *candour*, of *friendfhip*, of *integrity*, firft to leave out the chief claufe of an argument, and then to apply the argument to a fubject which you muft be *fure* that the writer of the argument never had in his eye? The texts I referred to you affert, "only declare what was done, but do not lay any injunction upon us." Let them be read, Sir. Read Ephef. v. 19. Col. iii. 16. Jam. v. 13. I wifh no more. You add "Or do you mean your matter and manner of finging are inculcated and

B enforced

enforced both by precept and example in the New Testament?" Good Sir, I meant what I said. Had I said any such thing? was it possible for you to suppose that I meant any such thing? " Perhaps, you mean singing simply considered, without any respect either to matter or manner." Perhaps I do, Sir. Perhaps no man but yourself could have put any other construction upon my words. You subjoin, " If this be your meaning, yet we are at a loss to know *what* and *how* to sing." To be sure. Because I expressly told you under that very head, that I deferred this subject till afterwards, (Diff. p. 23, 24. Reply, p. 26.)

I said, " Singing is evidently a gospel ordinance." You reply, " this, like what you have said before of its being inculcated both by precept and example stands without proof." Yet you had the proofs before your eyes, Mat. xxvi. 30. Mark. xiv. 26. Acts xvi. 25. 1 Cor. xiv. 15. Ephes. v. 19. Col. iii. 16. Jam. v. 13. What think you of this? And yet you " do not find that singing is at all commanded in the New Testament!" (Diff. p. 23. Reply, p. 27, 28. *In* p. 29. You " remind me that all Jewish men and women did not sing together in their temple worship." But you produce no authority for this assertion; and therefore, you cannot blame me for suspending my belief. If fair evidence of this can be produced, I should be glad to meet with it.
But

But supposing this should be true, of which I humbly think no man can give fair evidence; yet as the New Testament injunctions respecting this duty, are so general and indefinite, (of which afterwards) this appears to me a sufficient reason for Christians, in this instance, to differ from the Jews.

In p. 30, 31. You make a demand, which, as it is very fundamental in the controversy, undoubtedly deserves attention. The demand is, that I prove the word *sung* is in the original of Mat. xxvi. 30. Mark xiv. 26. *Sang* in the original of Acts xvi. 25. and *sing* in the original of Heb. ii. 12. and Jam. v. 13. because you " have met with " some very learned men, who say that those " words are not in the original, but were " added by the translators." There is an aukwardness in your manner of stating this difficulty, which I wish to cover, with many other similar ones, as much as possible. But I am persuaded, no learned man can pretend to say that the *Greek* words, which we render sing in these places, are not in the original; or that the *English* word sing is *added* in any one of the texts you refer to; because there is not the least colour for any such pretence.† The only dispute that appears

---

† It may possibly prevent uneasiness in many readers, whose situation and circumstances I pretty well know, to observe here, that after some pains taken in

pears to me possible, is, whether those Greek words be properly translated or not. I wish I could on this point give you satisfaction. It would be very easy, but I think very improper, to crowd this little piece with quotations. I will attempt to state the matter as clearly as I can; and, as I am not conscious of any mistake, so I here promise, that if any proper judge on the question shall observe any, and will point it out to me, I will cheerfully retract it.

In four of these passages, Mat. xxvi. 30. Mark. xiv. 26. Acts xvi. 25. Heb. ii. 14. the same Greek word is used. It is allowed on all hands, that this word sometimes signifies to *sing* properly, and sometimes denotes *praise*, without expressing the manner *how* that praise is offered to God, whether in a musical tone of voice, or otherwise. Some have thought the former, and others the latter, to be the *primary* signification of the word. But so far as I can judge, those of the former opinion are much more numerous, as well as more learned, than those

---

in this enquiry, I can assure them that it does not appear from *Mill. Wetstein,* or any other critic, that among all the various readings collected from different copies and manuscripts, there is a single various reading, in any of the places to which Mr. B. refers. Consequently, there is not the least foundation for a surmise that the word *sing* was added, in any one of the places, by our translators; but the fullest evidence to the contrary.

of

of the latter opinion. The word used in Jam. v. 13. is a different one, it sometimes signifies to make melody with instruments; but when applied to the voice, as it evidently is here, and in 1 Cor. xiv. 15. it properly signifies to sing, or make melody, as Ephes. v. 19, and never otherwise. On the whole, it appears to me, (1.) That the objection, if well founded, could not be of any great force in the present debate; because it is evident that singing is recommended in the New Testament, both by precept and example, if these passages were left out of the question. But then, it is clear to me, (2.) That these passages are full to the purpose; that the Greek word is properly rendered; and that the New Testament writers could not have used language more precise and full to enforce this practice of singing than they have used.

In p. 25. of my Dissertation, I attempted more directly to vindicate that method of singing which is generally used in Dissenting congregations. A great deal of what I said on this subject you have passed by, as if I had said nothing, though this part more particularly required your attention. Among other things, I observe that carnal people were allowed to join in singing formerly. This you do not deny; but you enquire, (p. 31.) when? or by whose authority?" I answer, I do not know that the blessed

God ever gave exprefs and particular rules refpecting the manner of conducting this or any other part of moral worfhip. But if the Divine Being had difapproved of it, we may very naturally fuppofe that he would have expreffed his difapprobation in this, as he does in other inftances. And the indefinite manner in which finging is recommended, even by David himfelf, (fee the following Differtation) is, with me, a fufficient argument that the bleffed God himfelf approved of it. Nor do I remember any intimation, either in the Old or New Teftament, that unconverted people ought not to fing the praifes of God. David appointed Heman, with his fourteen fons and three daughters; and twenty-three heads of families befides, with their fons and brethren; an exact number of every family, without any regard, that we read of, to their religious character, or fpiritual ftate. Now is it reafonable to fuppofe that thefe fathers and their children were all converted; or that David principally regarded their religious qualifications, when we have no hint of any fuch thing in the Bible?

I gave it as my opinion, that "finging in divine worfhip does not imply an immediate addrefs to God, arifing from prefent or paft fenfations; and expreffive of prefent or paft experiences;" and gave fome reafons for it. Thefe reafons again you pafs over, though

though under every obligation, in fair controversy, to examine them, and answer them if you were able. But instead of this, you say, "I must now tell you, that singing praises to God is an immediate address to him, as much as prayer on every solemn and special occasion." But, Sir, is your telling me this, a proof of it? And is your *Reply* to *me*, or to *yourself?* Did you not see that you had changed my expression from " singing in divine worship," to " singing praises to God?" With these hints I leave the reader to judge of your *candour, friendship,* and——but I *say no more.* (See Diff. p. 28. Reply, p. 31.)

I ventured, though with all the softness I could use, to observe, that I thought you had mistaken the meaning of Ephes. v. 19. Col. iii. 16. and endeavoured to prove it pretty largely. The proof you again overtook, and quote the words of Dr. Whitby, without shewing wherein the Doctor either differs from me, or agrees with you; without attempting to prove that the Doctor was right; take all for granted, and proceed on your old ground, as if all were firm as a rock. What will men of sense and conscience say to these things? (Diff. p. 29, 30, 31. Reply, p. 32, 33.

I endeavoured to prove that women have a right to sing the praises of God as well as men. If you had condescended to attempt a *reply* to my arguments, I think you would have felt the force of them. But I find I am not to expect this. You pick out four clauses, and tell me these conclude in your favour. But, as I do not understand you, I cannot answer you. The next page, you think is " quite weak," and as to my quotation from 1 Chron. xxv. 5, 6. you say, " what then? what have we to do with that?" I answer, Nothing, Sir, only to read it; and see whether it be not one out of many proofs, that " women have joined with men in singing." (Diff. p. 32—38. Reply, p. 37, 38.)

I am very sensible that instrumental was joined with vocal music in this instance, as well as others. But this subject I reserve to its proper place.

You allow of women speaking in the church " on certain just occasions;" but ought you not then to prove that singing in divine worship is not a *just occasion*, or else retract the opposition you have made against it from that topic? I had observed " there is no disorder in women joining with men in singing the praises of God, any more than there is when *men* jointly sing his praises; nor more than there is when both sexes join in prayer." You have mangled the argument in this manner, " there is no disorder in women joining with men in singing the
praises

praises of God, than there is when both sexes join in prayer. Again, leaving out the chief clause in the argument, and making me speak nonsense in the other part of it. I grant, while one is praying, the rest are silent; but is there any more *disorder* when many sing together, than when one prays, and the rest are silent? That is the question, according to the argument, even in its *mangled*, form: and you have not attempted to answer this question. (Diff. p. 38. Reply, 39, 40.)

In the nine following pages I meet with a great deal of— I beg to be excused from saying what. I am ashamed; I am grieved for you. However, as I cannot think *you* wish it to be considered as argument, I pass these pages over in silence.

In p. 50. you observe, "We read of Paul, and the other apostles, preaching in many places, especially Paul, but we no where read of him and the people to whom he preached, all singing together, or that they sung at all." Do we read of them *praying* together? Would you then prove from thence, that they did not pray at all? I grant also, that we never read of the churches singing together after they were settled. But we read as much of this as we do of their meeting together, to pray, or preach. Must we say there were no praying, nor preaching in their affemblies? It is the evident tendency of thefe arguments of yours, to put an end to all publick worfhip, though you are fo offended with me for mentioning this before, where I endeavoured to prove it more largely. (Diff. p. 49, 50. Reply, p. 53.)

When you exprefs your wonder why we do not ufe precompofed fermons and prayers, as well as precompofed pfalms and hymns. One reafon which I affigned is, "we have divine authority for precompofed pfalms and hymns; but not for precompofed fermons and prayers." The firft part of this you tranfcribe, the latter you *leave out.* — " I fay fo too," you reply. " But precompofed by who? And for whofe ufe, and how to be ufed?"—Now you muft fee here, Sir, that thefe circumftances were not in queftion, but belonged to another place. I was ftating an undeniable fact; that we follow fcripture examples in ufing precompofed pfalms and hymns, but not precompofed fermons and prayers. And as you admit the fact, this point is decided between us. I faid, " we have alfo a book of pfalms provided for us by our great Mafter in heaven." You reply, "*where* is that book?" You know we mean, the book of Pfalms: " and *what ufe* do you make of it." We fing it, Sir; you know we do;

and

and you know it was fung in the Jewifh church. I added, "We have not a book of fermons and prayers." "Yes, you have," fay you, "and equally as good a one as that of pfalms and hymns;" I do not know of it, nor ever heard of it. Pray inform me where it is. I affigned a third reafon. "There is alfo an evident propriety in the reafon of things, to prevent confufion in focial worfhip, in having precompofed pfalms and hymns, rather than precompofed prayers and fermons." You peremtorily deny it. "Not at all." How do you prove it? Why thus: "There is as much propriety in reading precompofed prayers and fermons, as in finging your precompofed pfalms and hymns." But do not you obferve, good Sir, that your conclufion has added three words to the argument, and omitted feveral, which gives it a different face? And how do you eftablifh your argument? "The former are the labours of men, and the latter are no more, and no other. And there may be as much divinity in the former, as in the latter, and equally ufeful and profitable." Now, I afk you, Sir, did not you read in the argument, "there is an evident propriety—to prevent confufion in focial worfhip?" I am forry to fay that thefe things cannot be hid. (Diff. p. 44. Reply, p. 51.) To proceed at this rate

rate would be almoſt endleſs. The contents of your fifty-ſecond, and following pages, we have already conſidered; and ſhall reſume the like ſubjects in the following diſſertation. That you may be abundantly happy in time and eternity, is the pleaſing hope, and ſincere prayer of your's affectionately,

D. TAYLOR.

P. S. Perhaps this may be a proper place to obſerve, that I do not think myſelf under any obligation at preſent to be concerned with *Philologus*. *Theophilus* can eaſily give him a ſufficient anſwer, if he think it neceſſary, without any aſſiſtance of mine. Who that gentleman is, I do not know, nor am I anxious to know. I have no inclination to offend him; but I truſt he will not charge it with impertinence, if I adviſe him to do *juſtice* to others, when he quotes their words, or refers to their writings. The reaſon of this advice is; he ſays Mr. T. *aſſerts* and *vows*, "that ſinging is eſſential to the ſtated worſhip of God," p. 12. Where has Mr. T. aſſerted any ſuch thing? Ought he not to have referred his readers to the page? If I had aſſerted any ſuch thing, I ſhould number it among the many miſtakes to which I confeſs myſelf daily liable, and ſhould here freely and publickly retract it. I do not remember that I ever

ever believed or thought any such thing. I do not believe it either of singing, praying, or preaching. I am persuaded there may be times of stated worship, when for sufficient reasons, any one of these parts of worship may be properly omitted. But I firmly believe that singing is as much essential to the stated worship of God as praying, or preaching.

A Second

A SECOND DISSERTATION ON SINGING IN THE WORSHIP OF GOD.

THE Rev. Mr. Boyce having published a reply to my *former* " differtation on finging in the worship of God," I venture again, to fubmit my thoughts to the public on this fubject, in the following propofitions; praying that the God of all wifdom and grace may be pleafed to direct both in writing and reading, and to make all terminate in the promotion of his own glory; and intreating my readers to beware of that four and malignant temper which fo naturally and fo frequently mingles itfelf with controverfy.

Propofition I. Whatever practice is enjoined in the Old and New Teftament, without any intimation that fuch practice is a pofitive inftitution; or defigned for extraordinary purpofes; or that it fhall afterwards be laid afide;—if this practice be at the same time, recommended in general and indefinite terms, to Christians, to men, to churches, without exception; and no particular qualifications required in order to perform it—this practice so recommended and enjoined, remains a duty in all succeeding ages.

I think all professed Christians will admit the principles contained in this proposition, and do, in general, act upon them. Nor do I see how the scriptures can be considered as a perfect rule of faith and conduct, nor how we can distinguish between right and wrong, or between moral and positive duties, if we deny these principles. If these were not *criteria* of moral and perpetual duty and obligation, the scriptures would rather perplex than instruct us; while we have the light in our hands, we should wander in darkness, and be left to mere reverie on the most important branches of duty both to God and man; I cannot but think that Mr. B. himself will grant all this. I therefore omit the formal proof of it.

Prop. II. *Singing the praises of God* is a duty recommended in the manner, and with the circumstances which have just now been mentioned; and consequently *singing the praises of God* is a duty of perpetual obligation; and the injunctions to practise it contained in scripture, are in force to all succeeding generations to the end of time.

We

We apply for proof of this, the several parts of the former proposition to the practice of singing.*

1. Singing the praises of God is frequently enjoined and recommended, both in the Old and New Testament. This is evident to all who read the Bible. Now if it had been enjoined in the Old Testament, and not in the New, we might have scrupled the practice of it at this day, with more appearance of reason. But the contrary is undeniable. A large number of passages may be found cited from both Testaments in proof of it, in the former dissertation (p. 8, 9.) As the inattention of many readers is astonishing, I here repeat what I there admonished the reader of, that I have now no design to treat of the *manner* of singing; but to prove that singing is a duty. I here further observe, that as Mr. B. on almost every occasion, introduces something relating to instrumental music, I reserve that

---

* I consider the subject in this manner, and with this latitude, because it is evident, that though Mr B. frequently speaks of " singing in the manner we do," yet some of his reasonings tend to overthrow the practice entirely at *this day*. (See Reply, p. 16, 55. &c.) And it is a known fact that several, who are of his opinion, have been offended to hear individuals sing in private, and have resented it very warmly. I mistake if it will not be generally found, that those who adopt his sentiments on this head, do not sing at all, either socially or separately.

subject

subject to be considered alone, in its proper place.

2. The practice of singing the praises of God is not only enjoined in the scriptures, but it is enjoined without any intimation that we are to consider it as a positive institution. There is no such intimation, that I recollect, in all the Bible. If there be, Mr. B. certainly ought to produce it, and we wish him to do it, that the debate may turn on its proper hinge. Positive institutions, under every dispensation, continue, from the nature of them, so long as the ends for which they were appointed continue needful to be answered. The two positive institutions of the New Testement, therefore, continue necessary to the end of time, because the purposes which they subserve in the Christian œconomy will always be necessary. These purposes are the lively representation of our blessed Saviour's death, burial, and resurrection, which can never be too thankfully remembered, or too strikingly represented. The positive institutions of the *Jewish* dispensations, for the same reason, were necessary, till the end of that dispensation, but no longer. Thus circumcision, for instance, was a token between the blessed God and the posterity of Abraham;* and the various sacrifices were " a shadow of good

* Gen. xvii. 11.

things to come" under the gospel.* But when the middle wall of partition between the Jews and Gentiles was broken down, the token of distinction was of no further use; and when the *substance* was come, the shadow might be conveniently dispensed with. Hence it appears, that if singing had been a positive institute of the New Testament, the perpetuity of it might have been argued from that consideration. But if it had been a positive institute of the Old Testament, it would have ceased at the commencement of Christianity. As it is, however, a duty common to both dispensations, enjoined and practised under both, the obligation to perform it, appears from hence, to be moral and perpetual. None can surely imagine that any practice is less incumbent on Christians, because it was observed by the Jews, unless it were designed to be confined to them. For if that could be proved, prayer and most other duties ought to be laid aside.

3. It will also appear to an attentive mind, that singing was not designed, under either dispensation, to serve uncommon or extraordinary purposes. On the other hand, the *reasons* assigned for it, the *motives* by which it is enforced, and the ends to be answered by it, are all moral and perpetual.

* Heb. x. 1.

Why

Why are other religious duties yet necessary, but from the authority by which they are enjoined, and the good moral purposes to be answered by them? Now if these arguments are valid in favour of other duties, why not in favour of singing? This practice, if I mistake not, will be found, on a careful examination, to be as frequently, and as forcibly recommended, from moral considerations, as most duties recommended in the Bible.

Consider the *reasons* and *motives* by which it is enforced; because it is *good*, *comely*, and *pleasant* *. These are invariably the same, so long as man is man. David would sing, *because* " God was his strength, and the God of his mercy, his defence and refuge in the day of trouble ‖." For the same reasons may every saint sing to the end of time. David exhorts others to sing the praises of God, *because* " he is a great God," a great King above all Gods, because he hath done marvellous things; *because* he hath made known his salvation; *because* his mercy is above the heavens, and his truth reacheth unto the clouds; because his dominion is over all the world; he dwelleth in Zion; he is the strength of his people, and the rock of their salvation; he taketh pleasure in his people,"—and so on.† These

---

* Psal. xcii. 1. cxxxv. 3. cxlvii. 1.   ‖ Psal. lix. 16, 17.   † See Psal. xcv. 1, 2, 3. xcvi. 2, 3, 4. cviii. 3, 4. xlvii. 6, 7.

considerations are exprefsly affigned as motives to enforce the duty of finging the divine praifes; and they are all moral, perpetual, and immutable, to the end of the world. Surely then the practice enforced by thefe confiderations muft be fo too, unlefs we have fome where authority to difcontinue this practice, or fome intimation that it ought to be difcontinued.

The *ends* to be anfwered by this practice are alfo moral, and of perpetual neceffity. To *fing* forth the honour of Jehovah's name, to make his praife glorious, to make a joyful noife before him, to fhew forth his falvation, to teach and admonifh ourfelves, or each other, and the like, are the purpofes for which this facred and delightful practice was appointed ‡.

Thus, I think, every confideration by which finging the praifes of God is recommended in fcripture, is moral and immutable. It is moft reafonable, therefore, to conclude that it is a moral duty, and never to be difcontinued.

It is granted that thefe reafons may be affigned for, and thefe ends are, at leaft, in a meafure, accomplifhed by prayer, preaching, and thankfgiving; and this is an unanfwerable argument to enforce thefe duties. But to make this confideration an objection againft finging for thefe purpofes,

‡ See Pfal. lxvi. 2. xcv. 1. xcvi. 2.

is

s to set up our own wisdom as superior to hat of our Maker. I add,

4. Singing the praises of God is enjoined and recommended in very indefinite and unlimited language; such language, as makes it appear that this practice ought not to be confined to any particular class of men, or to men of any particular description. Our knowledge of the manner in which divine worship was statedly performed among the Jews, or by the primitive Christians, is confessedly imperfect. It is certain, that in and after the time of David, the Jews had a select number or choir of singers. But it does not from hence necessarily follow, that none besides these were allowed to sing. Nor do I recollect any evidence that none were employed in this service, besides the Levites. Their being called singers is certainly no proof of it at all. For they would be so called, as being appointed to that office for the sake of having the service performed with more decency and order, even though the whole congregation joined with them. This is according to the common language of Christians. In most congregations some are appointed to lead the whole assembly in this service; but the whole assembly are supposed to join with them, if able to do it; and yet those, who lead the song, are emphatically called *singers*. It is, however,

ever, certain and undeniable, that singing is enjoined in very unlimited and indefinite terms in both the Old and New Testament, and this is sufficient for our present purpose. "Sing unto the Lord *all the earth* let the *nations* be glad, and sing for joy make a joyful noise unto the Lord *all y[e] lands*; all the kings of the *earth* shall praise thee. They shall sing in the ways of the Lord," and so on*. We need not enquire into the precise meaning of these passages. I am persuaded, that on every possible interpretation, they furnish proof that singing is not to be confined to men of any particular description. David himself was no Levite; yet he declares his determination to sing " while he has any being †."

Nor is this practice confined to any particular description of men in the New Testament. The apostle addresses the Ephesians and Colossians in the same general language, which he uses on all other occasions, to enforce any religious or moral duty whatsoever ‡. Let any one read the passages, and consider the connection in which they stand, and see if there be any kind of limitation or restriction expressed or implied in them. Let him try impartially whether he can find any argument

---

* 1 Chron. xvi. 23. Psal. lx. 4. xcvi. 1. c. 1, cxxxviii. 5. † Psal. civ. 33. cxlvi. 2. ‡ Eph. v. 19. Col. iii. 16.

prov

prove, that it is not as much the duty of all Christians to sing, as to redeem time, to avoid drunkenness, to be filled with the spirit, to give thanks to God, or to practise any other duty. The apostle James wrote a *general* epistle to the " twelve tribes, scattered abroad;" and to all these, without exception, he says, " Is any merry ? Let him sing psalms."*

Now how can we imagine that this practice would be recommended in this general and unlimited manner, unless it be a general duty, and incumbent in the same extent as other duties are ? When we find the fear of God, prayer to him, looking to him, and the like, so frequently recommended in scripture to all the earth, and all the ends of the earth, or recommended in other language, equally extensive and unlimited, what conclusion do we draw ? Certainly, that these duties are incumbent on all men. Why then should we not explain the passages which enjoin singing, as we explain all other passages where the same kind of language is used ? I only alledge,

5. That no particular capacities or qualifications are ever mentioned as requisite to the performance of this duty. Let all the passages before referred to, and all others, be examined with this view; and

* James v. 13.

I think it will strike every attentive mind, that what I here assert is true. Now if any reader shall please to consider, p. 21, 22, 23, 24, of the former dissertation, and what has been said in the foregoing pages of this dissertation, he may judge for himself whether we ought to esteem the practice in question a moral duty, and of general and perpetual obligation. Mr. B. indeed, says he, " can find no argument throughout my whole piece," to prove that singing is a moral duty, (Reply, p. 44.) But surely, he can find an attempt to prove it. Ought he not to have examined that attempt, and to have refuted it, if it had been in his power?

Prop. III. Frequent examples of the performance of any duty, by persons of different classes and descriptions, recorded in different parts of both the Old and New Testament, are justly considered as confirmations of that practice; and contribute to enforce it upon us as a perpetual and indispensable duty. If this were not allowed, a great part of the Bible would be a mere amusement. Because a great part of it consists of narration, and is evidently designed to inform us how the servants of God exerted themselves in former times, to glorify their Creator and Saviour. But if these narrations be not designed to influence our practice, and to excite in us a desire to
imitate

imitate the excellencies of these holy men, what end do they answer? They seem to be only matters of speculation, if not designed to have this effect. Besides, if this were not their design, the practice of all ministers is utterly wrong. Nothing is more common than to recommend and enforce duties which are enjoined elsewhere, by the examples of ancient saints, who were diligent in the performance of them. The good moral effect which this method has often had on all classes of men, is universally known. Nay, we have the authority of the apostles themselves for paying this regard to the examples of ancient saints, and are commanded to " be followers of those, who through faith and patience now inherit the promises *." If therefore, singing the praises of God be a duty thus enforced by example, this is a further consideration to excite our regard to it.

Prop. IV. Singing the praises of God is not only often enjoined, and strongly recommended, by moral arguments, but it is a practice of which we have many examples, both in the Old and New Testament †. It

---

* See Heb. vi. 12. James v. 10, 11. 1 Pet. iii. 6. and many other places.

† To proceed thus slowly, and express myself in so formal and familiar a manner, perhaps requires an apology with some persons who think the case very plain without a formal discussion. But the state of some who are likely to read these pages seems to me to render such a method necessary.

was practised by the people of Israel before the Jewish law was given ‡. And at Beer soon after the giving of the law *. It was practised by Deborah and Barak, in the time of the Judges †. By the Jews, in their public worship, in the days of David, and afterwards. This is clear from the Old Testament History throughout. It was also practised by our blessed Saviour and his apostles, at his last supper ‖; by Paul and Silas, in the prison at Philippi ‡, and by the Christian church at Corinth §.

The reader will here observe the different characters of those, who are mentioned as having been employed in this practice. So far as we can learn, the people of Israel, without exception, sang jointly, at the Red Sea, and at Beer; and this was both before and after the law was given. Afterwards, before the Levites were appointed to this office, Deborah and Barak sung; a woman and a man. After this service was assigned to the Levites, to be conducted by them, not only David the king *, but also of the Levites, Heman the seer, with his sons, and his daughters, and twenty three others,

---

‡ Exod. xv. I submit it to the judgment of thinking men, whether Exod. xv. and xxxii. 18. do not suggest a strong probability that this was a common part of worship even in the wilderness.

* Numb. xxi. 17.   † Judg. v.   ‖ Mat. xxvi. 30.   Mark xiv. 26.   ‡ Acts xvi. 25.   § 1 Cor. xiv. 15. 26.   * 2 Sam. xviii. 2.

with

with their sons and their brethren, twelve in every course, were employed in this delightful exercise †. Our blessed Saviour and his disciples, before the extraordinary gifts of the Spirit were given; two ministers, Paul and Silas, and the Corinthian church, after the bestowment of those gifts. So that we have clear scripture example of kings, governors, and the common people; of men and women; of young people of both sexes, and their parents; of our blessed Saviour, our perfect pattern, and his apostles, the planters and teachers of the Christian churches; and of one church of Christ in its settled state, who all practised singing in the worship of God.

Now in what manner are we accustomed to reason in other cases? We enforce prayer and other duties by precepts and examples. Why should not the duty of singing be enforced in the same manner? I beg leave here to repeat what I have hinted before; that I think, whoever will be at the pains of examining, will find that very few duties are more fully or more clearly inculcated in the Bible, both by precept and example, than singing the praises of God.

I may just observe here, that as Mr. B. strongly opposes women being permitted to sing in public worship, I endeavoured to

---

† 1 Chron. xxv. 6—31.

vindicate them in the former Differtation. Moſt of the arguments I uſed, Mr. B. paſſes by without taking any notice of them. As this is a capital branch of the controverſy, ſurely he ought not to have done ſo. The reader, if he chooſe, may examine what is ſaid on the ſubject. (Diſſ. p. 32— 41. Reply, p. 37—49.)

Prop. V. It is evident that ſeveral religious duties are enjoined and ſtrongly recommended in ſcripture, which are not expreſsly appointed to be performed in public worſhip, nor have we any particular directions as to the *manner* of performing them; and yet it is ſufficiently clear that they always have made a part of public worſhip; and muſt make part of it, otherwiſe we cannot ſee how public worſhip can be kept up in the world. For inſtance, it is not expreſsly enjoined that we ſhould pray or give thanks in public worſhip. But we know that theſe are parts of the worſhip of God, which may be advantageouſly introduced into his public worſhip; and we have ſufficient evidence that they have been ſo in all ages, even with the approbation, and by the direction of the Almighty. But if we go upon the ground of expreſs direction, we ſhall find no authority to perform them when we publicly aſſemble together. We can only practiſe them on the ſame ground on which we ſing the praiſes of God,

as

as I hope to prove more fully in its proper place.

For this reason I have said in the former Dissertation, and I here repeat it, that "if Mr. B's arguments be valid enough to annul the practice of singing, they are equally so to annul the practice of praying and preaching; and to demolish the whole fabric of public worship all together." Mr. B. denies this; but does not attempt to answer what I have said in proof of it. (See Diss. p. 49, 50. Reply, p. 53.) This he undoubtedly ought to have done. I am, however, well persuaded that neither he nor any other man can vindicate either praying, or thanksgiving, in public worship, on any other ground than that on which we vindicate singing. Nor is any other ground of vindication necessary.

The same may be said with regard to the *manner* of praying, preaching, or giving thanks, or of conducting any part of public worship whatever. Particular directions are not to be found; nor are they at all needful. Nor, in the present state of things, could they be observed, without such inconvenience as would throw the church, and the world into confusion, and make the forms of religion a burthen to the best of men. The slightest attention to the capacities, connections, and other circumstances of mankind, must convince any thinking and underftanding man, that a precife and univerfal attention to fuch particular rules in all the parts of worfhip, is morally impoffible. How far fuch precife rules were either given or obferved in the temple worfhip, cannot, I think, be exactly determined from the Bible. But fuppofing it could, there is a vaft difference between the conveniences and advantages of one fingle people, circumftanced as the Jews were, for the obfervance of fuch precife rules, and of all the churches fcattered abroad, throughout the Chriftian world. Befides, the Jewifh œconomy was the infancy of religion; but the Chriftian difpenfation is the advanced and mature ftate of it, as we are frequently taught by the apoftle. Precife rules, with regard to the punctilios of mode and form, are more needful in a ftate of infancy, than in advanced age. Every head of a family, who has children of different ages under his care, proves the truth of this daily. I add alfo, that the Jewifh religion was confeffedly a burthenfome one, which continually " gendered to bondage;" but the law of Chrift, compared with the Jewifh, is, in all refpects, a law of liberty, as far as it relates to modes and forms of worfhip. This appears on the very face of the apoftolic writings. Once more, it is an undeniable fact that different churches do conduct their public worfhip

differ-

differently, as to the *manner* of it, one from another. This is true even of those churches which are constituted in the same manner, and, on the whole, agree in the same kind and forms of worship, and are associated in the same connection. Nay, even the same church finds it necessary, on some occasions, to change the circumstances of worship, with respect to mode and form. This might be fully illustrated, if necessary, by instances, with respect to the parts of it, the frequency of any of these parts, the time of performing them; whether ministers shall preach, expound, or exhort; these, and a great number of other circumstantial things, must be determined by general rules, and the particular cases of the church or churches in question; because no particular rules are given by the Lord and head of the church.

Nor has all this the least tendency to encourage Popery, or please the Papists, as Mr. B. would insinuate; (p. 54.) nor does it give the least encouragement to introduce human inventions or any kind of will-worship into the church; nor authority to change any positive rite, or to vary from any direction which our blessed Lord has given; for all this is said on the supposition that the various parts of divine worship are exactly specified in scripture, and strictly enjoined on all professed Christians. Nor has any man licence to dictate to another; or to neglect any branch of worship which Christ has enjoined. And it is an admirable display of the wisdom and goodness of our dear Saviour, that the rules and directions of his word, respecting the affairs of his church, are circumstanced as they are. The use of this proposition will, I trust, be sufficiently manifest under the two following ones.

Prop. VI. When the particular manner of performing or conducting any part of religious worship is not exactly specified in scripture, it is reasonable, safe, and necessary to conclude that this is a matter of less importance, and may be sufficiently determined some other way; that is, by general rules, examples, the reason of things, analogy, conveniency, tendency to edify, or the like. To me it is evident, for the reasons already assigned, that this is the only method by which we are to determine the manner of conducting every part of public worship; and that every church, and every minister, ought to take this method, and to be very careful in observing it. As it has pleased the Lord to give us no particular directions on this head, we are, I think, under the necessity, either of laying public worship aside, which is directly opposite both to scripture and to common sense; or of performing it as we please, without any rule or regard to circumstances—or of performing it according to the dictates of human

man authority—or we must consider, by general rules and circumstances, what method is, on the whole, the best, and act accordingly.

Now the first of these cannot be admitted. We must not proceed as we please, in any thing which respects the interest of our blessed Lord and Saviour. That would be usurping an authority frequently condemned. Nor ought we to act by human authority; for that would be to flight our great Master, who has forbidden it, and to sacrifice his interest to the capricious humours and fancies of men; to disregard the *general* rules contained in his word, and to reduce ourselves to slavery, when he has made us free.—We must, therefore, proceed on the grounds before-mentioned.

The apostle has given us four general rules, to which, if we always diligently advert, we shall be safe. "Let all things be done to edifying—Let all things be done decently and in order—Do all to the glory of God—Let all your things be done with charity."† It is easy to observe, that these general rules would not have been given, nor wanted, if we had been furnished with particular ones; because they are evidently designed to supply the place of particular rules. It is also clearly supposed that the use of these, instead of particular rules, is

---

† 1 Cor. x. 31. xiv. 26. 40. xvi. 14.

perfectly sufficient, and will answer every valuable end. Now unless the conveniencies and edification of the churches, and particular members of them, be examined, and carefully attended to, things cannot be done "decently, in order, with charity, or to edifying." If this be not done, one is pleased, while another is disgusted; things are adapted to the conveniency of one, while heavy burthens lie upon others. This, I fear, is too often the case; and by these neglects in ministers, and leading members of churches, love is much diminished, general edification prevented; and the issue is frequently disorder and confusion.* I beg the reader's pardon for this digression. It may be of advantage in opening our way to

Prop. VII. As there are no particular directions given in scripture, *how* to conduct public worship in general; neither are there any such directions for the *manner* of conducting singing in particular. For the sake of some readers, it may be proper here to state a few facts, the evidence of which results from what has been said in the foregoing pages.

It is a *fact*, that public worship is a divine appointment, and has had the sanction

* I have ventured to give my thoughts more largely on these, and kindred subjects, in Consistent Christian, p. 121.-142, Diss. on Singing, p. 46, &c.

of

of divine approbation, under both the Old and New Testament dispensations.

It is a *fact*, that prayer, thanksgiving, and singing the praises of God, are all expressly appointed of God, and approved by him; and so far as we can learn, they have been so in all ages of the world.

It is a *fact*, that none of these several parts of divine worship are *expressly* commanded to be statedly performed in public worship.

It is a *fact*, that Mr. B. himself cannot pretend to vindicate his *manner* of conducting public worship by any *express* command of scripture.

It is a *fact*, that so far as we are able to learn, *all* these parts of worship, before mentioned, that is, prayer, thanksgiving, and singing, have been performed in *public* worship in all ages, and this with divine approbation.

It is a *fact*, that with respect to *express command*, singing in public worship is founded on the same authority, and accompanied with the same evidence, with which any other part of worship is accompanied, when performed in public.

Now as all professed Christians, those who are under the controul of human authority excepted, do consider it their duty to conduct their public worship, as to the *manner* of it, in all its branches, by general rules, examples, tendency to edify, and so on;

C 6   ought

ought not singing to be thus conducted, as well as every other branch of worship? Mr. B. allows, that singing is not " a scriptureless practice:" certainly then, it ought to be some way performed. That singing is as strictly enjoined as *forbearance, charity,* or any other duty, has, I think, been fully proved; and I should apprehend that it cannot be disputed by any who believes the New Testament.‡ Nor can I find any intimation that it is not to be continued to the end of time; but strong proof of the contrary. This we have seen already. We are therefore under indispensable obligation to practise it; and to enquire how it may be done in the most proper and profitable manner. It is evident, this can only be determined, as we determine the *manner* of conducting every other part of divine worship.

Let us take a view of the analogy in a few instances. Are we expressly commanded to sing in stated public worship? Not that I know of, unless Psal. cxlix. 1. or c. 1, 2. can be proved to contain such a command; on which I do not here insist. Are we expressly commanded to pray, preach, or give thanks in public worship? not that I remember. Have we examples of public prayer, preaching, giving thanks, and sing-

‡ Ephes. v. 15. 23. Col. iii. 13. 18. Jam. v. 13, &c.

ing

ing the praifes of God, among the Jews? Yes, all of them. Have we any examples in the New Teftament, of public finging in the primitive Chriftian church? I think not any, befides 1 Cor. xiv. though a confiderable argument might be formed on Acts iv. 24. But we need not reft any thing on probabilities here. Have we any other, or clearer examples of public prayer, preaching, or thankfgiving, in the primitive Chriftian church? I do not remember any. Are the ends to be anfwered by finging, and the motives to enforce it, moral, and of perpetual obligation? Yes; we have proved this before. And may we fay the fame of prayer, preaching, and thankfgiving? Yes, the very fame. Have we any particular directions, *how* to conduct or perform prayer, preaching, or thankfgiving, in public worfhip? No; not any more than for the *manner* of performing the practice of finging. Have we *general* rules, which apply equally to all thefe parts of worfhip? Yes; we have cited four of them. Prov. vi. Have we *occafional* directions with refpect to the *matter* of preaching, prayer, and thankfgiving? Yes, many, both in the Old and New Teftament; and fo we have refpecting the *matter* of what fhould be fung, in both Teftaments, cited before. Have we examples of *forms of addrefs* proper for preaching, prayer, and thankfgiving? Yes, many, and fo we have

with

with respect to singing. See Prop. II. IV.*
As it has pleased God to enjoin prayer to him, fear of him, and other duties on men, sometimes in general and indefinite language, and at other times more particularly on his people; so he has likewise enjoined the practice of singing, in the same indefinite language, Prop. II. It is evident therefore, that singing the praises of God stands on the same ground with other religious duties.

As it has pleased our Creator to make us rational beings, we certainly ought to use

---

* Here may be a proper place to drop a hint respecting Hebrew poetry, about which Mr. B. seems to scruple (p. 49.) if it had been disputed two hundred and fifty years ago, whether "the psalms were written in Hebrew verse," or no, it would have been less wonderful. But that any man of understanding and reading should call it in question at this day, would hardly have been expected. "That the book of psalms, with some other writings of the Old Testament, were originally written in metre, is universally allowed by the Jews, and does also appear from the different accentuation of them from that of other books." Dr. Gill's Sermon on 1 Cor. xiv. 15. p. 47. 2d. edit. "Have they forgot, or were they never told, that many parts of the Old Testament are *Hebrew* verse? and the figures are stronger, and the metaphors bolder, and the images more surprizing and strange, than ever I read in any profane author." Watts's Lyric Poems, pref. p. 8. 7th edit. The present bishop of London has placed this subject in a very clear and strong light, in his fine prælections upon it; and in his Preliminary Dissertation, prefixed to his new translation of the prophet Isaiah.

our reason in performing what he has commanded; not in opposition to his word, but in subjection to it. Now reason tells us singing is a social exercise; and (allowing it to be right) may be performed jointly, without any confusion, irregularity, or disadvantage whatever: nay, that by performing it with joint voices, the ends designed by it may be answered, better than when performed separately, by individuals. This, all impartial men will acknowledge; and both scripture, and the experience and practice of all mankind, avouch the truth of it: this, therefore, is one circumstance strongly in favour of singing with joint voices. But it cannot be said of any other part of divine worship. It cannot be denied that *all* are under obligation to praise God; and where is the impropriety, or moral turpitude of doing it with a modulated voice? But I add, both reason and scripture shew, that all mankind ought to employ every capacity in the service of God; and therefore, the voice, as well as other capacities. It is certain that women, and children, who are come to understanding, are able to use their voices in shewing forth the praises of God, as well as others. They therefore ought to do it, unless the scripture forbid them, or contain that which implies a prohibition of them. What right have we, without scripture warrant, to forbid them, or dissuade
them

them from it? If spiritual songs be composed on other subjects, besides immediate addresses of praise to God, of which kind we find many in scripture; women, and unconverted people, can think on these subjects, and be profited by them; and constant experience shews that poetry and singing are useful to the contemplative powers of man. Is it then reasonable that they should be deprived of this advantage which the God of nature hath given them? We have certain evidence, in fact, that this exercise hath been useful in many instances, to women and children; even unconverted, as well as converted. Reason and experience therefore strongly plead that they should be allowed and encouraged to practise it. It is granted that all this would not be absolutely decisive, supposing they had no encouragement from scripture to attend to this sacred exercise. I therefore add, that we have clear evidence, that women and unconverted people have joined in this service, and we cannot find that their doing so was at all displeasing to God; but good reason to believe the contrary.* We have likewise proved before, that this practice is enjoined on all the earth, without exception. Is it right then for us to oppose it,

* See Exod. xv. Numb. xxi. Judg. v. 1 Chron. xxv.

against reason, experience, scripture precept, and scripture example?

In my former Dissertation, some of these things were mentioned, which I have here endeavoured to amplify. Ought not Mr. B. to have fairly examined what is there said on the subject? With respect to the spirituality of worship, and the unacceptableness of it, when performed by unconverted people, no objection can be offered on this head, that I am able to conceive, but what equally militates against their reading, praying, hearing, and every other duty they perform. Nay, I think, whoever can prove from these topics, that they ought not to sing the praises of God, will be able to prove from the same topics, and with equal evidence, that they ought to attend to nothing, either in sacred or civil life; but that they all ought to lie down and die. Because, till they believe in Jesus, "be renewed in the spirit of their mind," and act from the obedient spirit which the gospel inspires and produces, whatever they do, it cannot be pleasing to God. But this can be no argument against their performing religious duties of moral obligation; for then it would be no sin to neglect them; and if so, it would follow, by an easy and obvious method of reasoning, that unconverted persons are not sinners. I think, if Mr. B. choose to try his strength on what is is said under the second and fourth propositions, he will find it sufficiently evident, that singing the praises of God is a duty enforced on persons of all characters; and consequently, no valid argument can be formed against unconverted people being found in the practice of it. I suggested this hint in the former Dissertation; and he has taken some notice of it; but in such a manner, as I heartily wish, for his own sake, could be buried in oblivion. Diff. p. 31. Reply, p. 45.

As to the *place* where persons ought to sing: we have seen that singing is a social exercise, and has in all ages been so considered, and so performed. The examples of it in scripture are very numerous; and these both in the Old and New Testament. Now how can people perform it as a social exercise, unless when they assemble for divine worship, and perform other acts of social religion, which are enforced by the same considerations, and designed for similar purposes; such as prayer, thanksgiving, reading, expounding, preaching, and hearing the word, for mutual instruction and edification? Reason itself, therefore, demonstrates the propriety of public singing, as well, and on the same ground, as other public religious duties. And that we have abundant examples of public congregational singing is undeniable. It is true, these are

chiefly

chiefly in the Old Testament. For in the New, we have no account, that I know of, (unless it can be gathered from 1 Cor. xiv.) of the manner in which the Christians conducted their public worship, though we have abundant authority for the performance of it.

The most circumstantial account which we have in the New Testament of the *manner* of conducting social worship, is, I think, that of our Saviour and his disciples, after the institution of the Lord's supper. We are there distinctly informed that our Saviour delivered a most instructive and animating discourse, contained in the fourteenth, fifteenth, and sixteenth chapters of John's gospel; and in Luke xxii. 5—38. He then offered up a most affectionate prayer; (John xvii.) and he and his disciples at the same time sung a hymn. In this account, the three parts of worship are particularly mentioned; the preaching or instruction, and the prayer, expressly ascribed to our Saviour alone; and the singing to him and his disciples.* Perfectly agreeable to the practice of all ages, in which singing, so far as we can learn, has always been, in ordinary cases, accounted a social exercise, and performed as such, when performed in public worship.

* Psalm c. 2. 4.   cxlix. 1.

I may

I may add, we have not only clear scripture examples of public congregational singing, but also, scripture precept or exhortation. "Serve the Lord with gladness, come *before his presence*, into his public worship, with *singing*." "Sing unto the Lord a new song, and his praise in the *congregation* of saints." † I am utterly at a loss to understand the meaning of these passages, unless they are so to be understood. I think it will appear to any candid mind, that though Ephes. v. 19. Col. iii. 16. are not necessarily referred to public worship; yet the directions there given may be as properly applied to it, and as advantageously observed in it, as any other way whatever. To which I only add, that in all the public worship mentioned in the Bible, singing appears to have made a principal part.

Again, As to the *matter* of sacred song. We have seen already that singing is a social exercise, and has ever been practised with joint voices. Now *precomposed* songs

---

† It is well known that different harmonizers give the singing of the hymn different situations, with regard to time and place, in the service of that evening. But this is a question foreign to the present debate. The circumstances pertinent to our present purposes are, that our Saviour gave the instructions and prayed; but they (i. e. he and his disciples) sung the hymn. Nor can any thing be well made more fully evident by words than that singing was here performed as a social exercise, with joint voices.

are

are properly adapted to such an exercise as this, and necessary to the performance of it. We cannot conceive how it is morally possible that any number of persons should be able to compose and sing the same spiritual songs *extempore*. An attempt of this kind would be attended with intire confusion. Mr. B. seems to take it for granted, that in the church at Corinth only one person sung at once, that he composed and sung *extempore*; and that no other kind of singing was practised in that age. But I do not think any man can prove this. The other passages where singing is mentioned in the New Testament appear to be all of them clearly opposite to this hypothesis. Nor does it appear to me, that 1 Cor. xiv. furnishes any evidence that this was the practice of that church, even in the particular case to which the apostle there refers. But admitting that this was practised on some occasions, for some extraordinary purposes, which I do not wish to deny, such a practice could never be extended to all succeeding ages. These extraordinary gifts and uncommon performances were, at least in a great measure, peculiar to that age. Much less can this be improved into an argument for the discontinuance of singing in public worship; because that would militate against all the parts of divine worship, since they were all often performed ed by extraordinary gifts in the apoftolic age. This we have feen before.

That prayer is performed *extempore*, can be no proof that finging ought to be fo performed. Becaufe prayer arifes from the prefent ftate of the mind, and the prefent circumftances of ourfelves or others. But finging is, in this refpect, very different, and is not defigned to exprefs our prefent fenfations, or to arife from the circumftances, with which we or others are attended: but to recite, or ruminate on, the works, or will of God, in an agreeable and harmonious manner for the folace, inftruction, or admonition of others or ourfelves. This is manifeft from the book of Pfalms, as well as from feveral parts of the Old and New Teftament. This I endeavoured to demonftrate in the former Differtation. (p. 41, &c.) Mr. B. ought to have difproved it, if he had been able; or, if not, to have admitted the truth of it.

It is alfo a certain *fact*, that we have fcripture examples of precompofed pfalms and fpiritual fongs; but not of precompofed prayers or fermons to be ufed in divine worfhip. To fay thefe precompofed fongs were *infpired* is no argument in the prefent cafe. The difcourfes of the prophets and apoftles were infpired; but they were not precompofed for others, as the pfalms of David, Afaph, and others were. (Diff. p. 41.)

The

The reason is obvious. Precomposed songs were necessary, from the very nature of that part of divine worship; but precomposed sermons and prayers were not so, but improper, and would rather defeat than promote the designs of preaching and praying. I beg leave to add, that it is likewise an incontrovertible fact, though Mr. B. positively denies it, that we have in scripture a book of psalms, written for us by *inspiration of God*; but not a book of sermons and prayers. A plain intimation this, in favour of precomposed psalms and hymns. (See Diff. p. 44. Reply, p. 51.)

As to the objection made against *human* compositions, it is evident that we ought to use other words than those of scripture in prayer, thanksgiving, and preaching; and if so, why not also in singing? There is the same necessity for it, and the same good ends may be answered by it in the one case, as in the others. Mr. B. will perhaps answer again, that this "why not is not worth his notice." But I am well satisfied it is so much to the purpose in hand, that he will never be able to give a fair reply to it.

We certainly ought to make the best use we can of the word of God in our sermons and prayers; and so we ought in singing. Yet our preaching and prayers are *human* compositions, as well as our songs. There may be defects in our songs, as well as in our

our sermons and prayers. But that can be no proof that we ought to sing scripture language only, any more than that we ought to use no other language in prayer and preaching. If the reader please he may see other observations on this subject in the former Dissertation, (p. 41—46.) To have considered these were certainly the part of a *candid*, *friendly*, *fair* disputant. How far Mr. B. has attempted it may be seen in his Reply, (p. 49—52.)

Prop. VIII. It is very natural and reasonable to conclude, that *instrumental music* in divine worship is not of perpetual obligation, nor ought to be encouraged under the gospel; because it is not recommended in the manner in which other parts of divine worship are, nor attended with the evidence with which they are attended. Nor can it be vindicated by the arguments which may fairly be urged in favour of singing the praises of God. The difference is very considerable in several respects.

It is not once enjoined or recommended, or even mentioned in the New Testament; yet singing is enjoined there several times. We have several examples of singing, and even of *social* singing, in the New Testament; yet not one of instrumental music. The Psalmist speaks of singing as better, and more pleasing to God than sacrifices.* But

* Psal. lxix. 30, 31.

I do

I do not remember a hint of this kind respecting inftrumental mufic. Inftrumental mufic is not recommended for the moral purpofes of *teaching* and *admonition*, nor capable of fubferving thefe purpofes, as finging the praifes of God is. Nor is it enjoined in the fame indefinite and general language in which finging is enjoined. We cannot learn that inftrumental mufic in the worfhip of God was ever recommended to all men, or practifed by them; whereas we have feen above, that finging the praifes of God is exprefsly recommended to believers in general, to all Ifrael, to all the earth. It is therefore natural to confider it as peculiar to the former fhewy difpenfation, and defigned to ceafe when that difpenfation ended. If any man could produce the fame arguments in favour of inftrumental mufic, which are produced in favour of finging, I, for my part, fhould think it my duty to plead for it. On the other hand, if that could be faid againft finging, which can fairly be faid againft inftrumental mufic, I would decline all attempts to vindicate it. At prefent, I am fully perfuaded that finging the praifes of God is a part of moral worfhip, and an ordinance of Jefus Chrift, to be perpetuated to the end of time; and that nothing can fairly be pleaded in favour of inftrumental mufic, as a part of Chriftian worfhip, more than in favour of circumcifion, or any other

D   Old

Old Testament rite. To which I take the liberty of adding, it is of considerable weight with me, that singing the praises of God was practised in the first ages of the Christian church, after the time of the apostles. Even prejudice itself can hardly dispute the truth of this. Whereas musical instruments were not introduced into Christian worship till the very darkest ages of popery. This the Papists themselves are constrained to admit.*

Mr. B. frequently introduces this subject in his late *Reply*; with what propriety the reader will judge. He roundly and repeatedly charges me with partiality and disobedience; because I have ventured to plead for singing the praises of God; yet given my voice against instrumental music in divine worship. That these heavy charges should fall upon *me*, is, to be sure, a mere trifle; and so I hope to be enabled always to consider it. But when it is remembered, that they equally affect so great a part of the Christian world, in all nations, and in all ages; and such multitudes of the greatest, wisest, and best of men, of all distinctions—I leave the reader to judge of that man's modesty by whom they are exhibited. Did not our Saviour and his apostles prac-

* See Peirce's Vindication of Dissenters, Part III. p. 105, &c.

tife and recommend finging? Did they ufe or encourage inftrumental mufic? Does not this partiality and difobedience, therefore, originate with them?

But I forbear.——

" Why will you venture," fays Mr. B. (p. 10.) " to put afunder thofe things which are fo clofely joined together?" (i. e. finging and inftrumental mufic?) It is fufficient to anfwer, why did not our Lord and his apoftles join thefe together? why did they put them afunder? Was not this a plain intimation that they were defigned to be put afunder at the commencement of Chriftianity? Does he not know that inftrumental mufic is effentially diftinct from vocal? Are they not continually diftinguifhed in fcripture, and even in his Reply?— Did not the Jews burn incenfe at the time of prayer? Why does not Mr. B. join incenfe and prayer now? I know he hath a fufficient anfwer ready; and the fame anfwer will ferve in the cafe of inftrumental and vocal mufic. Can he vindicate inftrumental mufic by the fame arguments which are ufed in favour of finging in divine worfhip? If he can, he certainly ought; if not, there is a good reafon for adopting the one, and laying afide the other.

If inftrumental mufic were effential to finging, Mr. B's flourifh in his poftfcript would have been to his purpofe. But as

D 2 they

they are essentially distinct, and always distinguished, the case is entirely different from that supposed in my argument. Nevertheless, I here, with pleasure, embrace an opportunity, for which I have wished almost ever since my Dissertation was published, of acknowledging that the word *prohibition*, in the passage which he cites, may perhaps be too strong. Possibly *intimation*, or some such word as that may be preferable: and I wish the passage to be understood as here corrected, (Diff. p. 27, 28. Reply, p. 63, 64.)

I think it right, however, to call the reader's attention to Mr. B's manner of quoting the words of his antagonist. He omits a clause in my argument, on which the force of it chiefly rests. My words are, " on the same foundation it may be incontestibly argued in favour of promiscuous singing. This was practised in the worship of the Old Testament. Singing is still enjoined," &c. Mr. B's quotation is, " on the same foundation it may be incontestibly argued in favour of singing.—Singing is still enjoined," &c. Mr. B. leaves out the chief clause in my argument, " this (promiscuous singing) was practised in the worship of the Old Testament." By this mean the force of my argument is lost in his quotation of it. He has taken similar methods on other occasions; but I take no pleasure

pleasure in collecting the instances of this kind, nor in exposing any man for such conduct. The cause of truth appeared to me to require this hint, that the unwary reader may not be imposed on with false glare.

I wish not to ascribe any thing to wrong design in Mr. B. That is neither my province, nor my inclination. May the presence of God be with him continually, and with every other man who is a friend of truth, and a servant of Christ! I have given my advice more largely with respect to the *manner* of singing in divine worship in the former Dissertation. As *mere advice*, I still submit it, with deference, to every minister, and to every church of Christ. May the blessing of God accompany this, and the former Dissertation, for the glory of his own great and adorable name! Amen.

FINIS.

(Lately Published, by the same Author)

I. A Dissertation on Singing in the Worship of God; interspersed with occasional Strictures on the Rev. Mr. Boyce's late Tract, entitled, "Serious Thoughts on the present Mode and Practice of Singing in the public Worship of God." 6d.

II. The Necessity of searching the Scriptures; with Directions. A Sermon. 2d.

III. The Faithful and Wise Steward. A Sermon, addressed to young Ministers at an Association. 6d.

IV. The Mourning Parent comforted. The Substance of two Sermons, occasioned by the Death of two of the Author's Children. 4d.

V. The Scriptural Account of the Way of Salvation; in two Parts. 1s.

VI. Fundamentals of Religion in Faith and Practice. The Substance of Fifty Sermons. 3s.

VII. The Duty of Gospel Ministers explained and enforced at an Ordination; with a Discourse to the People, by the Rev. Mr. Thompson, of Boston. And an Appendix, respecting Church Fellowship; extracted and translated from Dr. Ames. 1s.

VIII. An Humble Essay on Christian Baptism; in which the Meaning of the Original Word, the Customs of the Jews, and the Sentiments of the Ancient Fathers respecting that Ordinance, are impartially considered. The Second Edition. With two Letters to the Rev. Dr. Addington, on the Subjects and Mode of Baptism. 1s.

N. B. The Letters to Dr. Addington, may be had separate. 3d.

IX. The Consistent Christian. The Substance of Five Sermons. 1s.

X. Our

X. Our Saviour's Commission explained and improved. A Sermon on Matt. xxviii. 19, 20. 4d.

XI. SCRUTATOR's Query, respecting the Extent of our blessed Saviour's Death, Reproposed, &c. 1d.

XII. SCRUTATOR to RESPONSOR; or, an Introduction to a farther Proof, (if need be) that Jesus Christ laid down his Life for the Sins of all Mankind. In two Letters to RESPONSOR, with a short Letter to CONSIDERATOR. The Second Edition. 2d.

XIII. Scripture Directions and Encouragements for Feeble Christians. Third Edition. 2d.

XIV. Rules and Observations for the Enjoyment of Health. Extracted from Dr. CHEYNE. 2d.

XV. Candidus examined with Candour. On Free Communion. 2d.

XVI. A Practical Improvement of the Divinity and Atonement of Jesus, attempted in Verse. 1s.

XVII. A Catechism; or Instructions for Children and Youth. Third Edition. 3d.

XVIII. Entertainment and Profit united Easy Verses on the chief Subjects of Christianity; for Children and Youth. Third Edition. 1d.

XIX. Observations on the Rev. Mr. FULLER's late Pamphlet, entitled, " The Gospel of Christ worthy of all Acceptation." In Nine Letters to a Friend. 9d.

XX. The Stroke of Death, practically improved. A Funeral Sermon for Mrs. SUSANNA BIRLEY, late Wife of the Rev. Mr. BIRLEY, of St. Ives, Huntingdonshire. To which is prefixed the Speech delivered at her Interment, by the Rev. Mr. ROBINSON, of Cambridge. 9d.

XXI. An Essay on the right Use of Earthly Treasure, in Three Letters to a Friend. Second Edition. 2d.

XXII. A Charge and Sermon, together with a Confession of Faith, delivered at the Ordination of the Rev. Mr. GEORGE BIRLEY, on Wednesday, October 18, 1786, at St. Ives, Huntingdonshire. The Charge, by D. TAYLOR, of London; the Sermon, by R. ROBINSON, of Cambridge. 1s.

XXIII. A Charge and Sermon, delivered at the Ordination of the Rev. Mr. JOHN DEACON, on Wednesday, April 26, 1786, at Leicester; together with the Introductory Discourse, the Questions proposed to the Church and the Minister, the Answers returned, and Mr. DEACON's Profession of Faith. The Introductory Discourse, and Charge, by D. TAYLOR, of London; the Sermon, by W. THOMPSON, of Boston. 1s. 6d.

Sold by J. BUCKLAND, Pater-noster Row; and B. ASH, No. 15, Little Tower-Street.

www.ingramcontent.com/pod-product-compliance
Lightning Source LLC
Chambersburg PA
CBHW020730100426
42735CB00038B/1456